SUMMARY

Seismic cultural and political shifts are under way in the Arab Gulf monarchies. The political upheavals and transitions that have swept through the Arab world over the last 2 years have not toppled the Arab Gulf rulers, but did not leave them untouched either. Rulers of Gulf Cooperation Council (GCC) states face heightened internal and external challenges and uncertainties. Pro-democracy protests and calls are extending from Bahrain to other oil-rich countries of the Arabian Peninsula. The expectations of GCC citizens, particularly the educated youth, are increasingly moving from socio-economic demands to political ones. They are now not only asking for jobs or wage increases, but also for more political participation and accountability.

Chief among internal challenges is the resurgence in several GCC countries, particularly Bahrain and Saudi Arabia, of a decades-long sectarian rift between the Sunni regimes and their Shia subjects. The Gulf regimes' already tense relations with Iran have worsened on the basis of alleged Iranian interference inflaming sectarian tensions in Bahrain and across the broader region.

In this monograph, the author assesses the challenges facing the region's rulers, and proposes meaningful political reform as a means of mitigating them.

THE FUTURE OF THE ARAB GULF MONARCHIES IN THE AGE OF UNCERTAINTIES

At first glance, the member states of the Gulf Cooperation Council (GCC),[1] with the exception of Bahrain, appear to have weathered the storm of the Arab uprisings with little visible disturbance. A closer look at the region, however, suggests that its perceived stability may very well be threatened in the longer term. This is because many of the region's government policies that are intended to appease their local populations — specifically the expansionary budgets and generous welfare and employment packages of the past 24 months — are intrinsically short-term solutions to wider and longer term social, economic, and political grievances that characterize the GCC economies as a whole.

In particular, GCC citizens expect long-term institutional reforms and more political freedom. Voices calling for more good governance, transparency, and an inclusive political system are increasing and spreading across the region. There are also concerns over the sustainability of many economic policies in the region, which raises the question of how sustainable current living standards will be.

The repercussions of the uprisings in several Arab countries in the Gulf region are multiple. They include the reviving of democratization demands, the potential of setting precedents of democratic models, and the weakening of Egypt as an important security partner. It would therefore be misleading to believe that the Arab Gulf monarchies will remain resilient indefinitely to the political awakening in several Arab countries. The GCC states also face various other regional and geopolitical challenges that further threaten the wider region's stability. For this reason, the Gulf monarchies' current equilibrium may well be of a short-term nature.

INTRODUCTION

Political upheavals across North Africa and the Middle East in 2011-12 brought seismic shifts in the geopolitics of the Arab world and in the internal politics of the entire region. The GCC countries, with the notable exception of Bahrain, succeeded in largely avoiding mass protest movements as observed in many other parts of the Arab world. But the Gulf monarchies nevertheless did not remain unaffected; small protest movements appeared in Kuwait, Oman, and other GCC states and managed to create a near-political crisis in Bahrain in early 2011. Many of the GCC states have since handed out generous welfare and employment packages — in many cases on top of already extremely generous welfare state functions — in order to appease demands by the populace for a greater share in their countries' wealth.

But the GCC states constitute a mosaic of countries facing much underlying — and until now unresolved — social, geopolitical, and economic conflict potential, including both domestic and external threats to their long-term stability. Internally, a combination of ethnic, political and economic factors is threatening the future of the political regimes in some GCC countries more than others. On the economic front, the region needs to create nonhydrocarbon sources of economic growth, which could translate into creating job opportunities for millions of young job-seekers across the GCC states. The influx of foreign labor over the economic boom years has contributed to the economic development and prosperity of the GCC countries, but many nationals continue to fail to match job requirements, while the disproportionate number of rootless foreigners has become a source of concern to the region's small states.

Sectarian tensions have been a concern to the GCC states for many decades. In recent months, accusations of an Iranian role in inciting sectarian tensions in several GCC states have been dominating headlines and public discussions across the GCC countries. Regardless of the accuracy of such accusations, the GCC Sunni regimes have increased their surveillance of the Shia population, while Bahrain's Shiite majority made a determined statement early in 2011 regarding their expectations of future access to the micro-state's wealth and political power. The media war is heightening tensions between Shia and Sunni populations in Bahrain and Saudi Arabia and affecting other GCC countries. These tensions, if not contained, could pose a threat to the social fabric and the region's stability.

Iran also remains the main external threat to the territorial integrity and interests of most GCC countries. Iranian-GCC tensions have had a long history, reaching back to the first two Gulf wars, and have arisen anew in recent years over a variety of issues including territorial disputes between the United Arab Emirates (UAE) and Iran, Qatar's and Iran's shared gas field in the offshore Gulf, and Iran's ongoing conflict with the West over its nuclear program. In the event of a military confrontation between Western states and Iran, the GCC states, which share Iran's main access route for its oil and natural gas exports, the Straits of Hormuz, would be exposed to significant disruptions of their main trade route regardless of whether they were involved in the conflict.

Of the several distinct challenges that are facing this part of the Arab world, internal problems remain the most difficult. The people of the region are increasingly demanding a change in the current conservative political systems. For decades, GCC rulers escaped introducing substantial political and economic reforms that could reduce their broad political powers.

Several initiatives have been announced by a number of GCC states at both national and regional levels to strengthen GCC security and resilience. For example, Saudi Arabia sees the establishment of a union among all the six members of the GCC as a strategic response to the growing assertiveness of Iran—a view that is not supported by all GCC members.

This analysis aims to answer the key question on the future of the Arab Gulf Monarchies in the face of these increasing internal and external challenges and threats. It is based on several months of research, including in the region itself, and includes the valuable input of more than 20 interviews conducted with decisionmakers both within and outside the region. Given the socio-political differences that persist among the GCC countries, an in-depth discussion of each country's domestic politics would be desirable; but in the light of space constraints, this monograph focuses on selected political issues that are common to the majority of GCC countries. However, the analysis will place more emphasis on Saudi Arabia given its size and influence in the region. What happens in Saudi Arabia matters in the rest of the GCC states, and undoubtedly, changes in Saudi Arabia are more likely to have repercussions on the rest of its GCC neighbors. The discussion will show that concerns about the future of the GCC monarchies are not an exaggeration. It would be misleading to believe that the Arab

Gulf monarchies will remain resilient to the political awakening across Arab countries. To prevent a repetition of uprisings seen in early 2011 in Tunisia and Egypt, it is essential that GCC states adopt substantial political reforms.

This monograph is divided into two main sections: the first covering internal challenges to GCC stability; and the second covering external challenges to the security and stability of the Arab Gulf countries overall. A conclusion reviews the potential impacts on U.S. interests.

PRECARIOUS STABILITY AT HOME

Threats from within remain the main concern to the stability of GCC regimes. This is not a novelty in the region. Over recent decades, the most serious threats to regime stability and security have been internal. The Iraqi invasion of Kuwait in 1990 remains the only serious external threat to any GCC regime in recent history.

The political upheavals of the last 2 years in the Arab world have introduced new challenges and brought dormant tensions to the fore. The list of threats to GCC regimes is wide-ranging, including factors affecting the cohesion of the social fabric of the GCC societies such as terrorism and demands for constitutional reform.

Increasing Calls for Democratization.

The GCC monarchies have not faced strong popular demands for democracy during their years of existence. Calls for democratization, at least in Saudi Arabia, have been on the agenda only for a limited circle of reformist elites. For the small rich countries, democracy has been an alien culture. For decades, the vast majority of GCC citizens were uninterested in their political systems or political participation in them. Only a tiny educated minority was involved in any kind of political activism. In countries such as Bahrain and Kuwait, where the political systems allowed limited formal political participation, a small number of young nationals showed interest in civic and political activities. But all this is now set to change.

Economic, educational, and technological advances over the last decades have rapidly changed how GCC nationals see their rulers and the management of their public affairs. The internet and social media have allowed GCC nationals to access information and political analysis to an extent that has never been allowed by local media and academia. The spread of democratic concepts across the region over the last decade through education and access to information has fundamentally altered assumptions and preconceptions there. An increasing number of people, mainly youth, sees in democratic political systems the most appropriate forms of government. A survey conducted in March 2011 showed that 60 percent of the GCC youth who took part in the survey considered democracy to be their top priority.[2]

At the time of this writing, political freedoms remain restricted in the region. All GCC regimes ban political parties, with the result that there are none in any GCC countries, including in Kuwait, which has a political system that resembles most closely some features of Western democracy. Kuwait and Bahrain have held parliamentary elections, but have political associations rather than political parties. Both countries allow women to vote and stand in elections.

Their parliaments have limited powers to oversee the executive body, which is dominated by members of the ruling family. Both parliaments possess blockade powers, but limited legislative power.

Despite some differences that characterize the formal politics, there are several key commonalities among the Arab Gulf monarchies. A distinguishing feature is the lack of any check and balance control on the powers of the Gulf monarchs. Another distinguishing feature compared to other Arab countries, including the monarchies of Jordan and Morocco, is that the GCC sovereigns rule as a family. Their family members are appointed to key positions and benefit from many privileges. The result is an increased susceptibility to political volatility, with the risk of unpredictable successor regimes. Although the system of government practiced by Jamal Mubarak in Egypt differed from that of the GCC states, at the time of this writing, Egypt provides a case in point demonstrating the potential complications of regime change.

The events of the Arab uprisings that started in December 2010 have revived demands for more inclusive and transparent politics in the GCC. "Days of Rage" were announced in almost every GCC country, emulating the calls to mass protests in North Africa. Bahrain and Oman are the countries that have seen large and continuous protests since early 2011. Bahrainis and Omanis, inspired by upheavals elsewhere, were the first to take to the streets to demand jobs, action against corruption, and other social and political reforms. In Bahrain, the political crisis was extremely complex, and political dialogue between the Sunni government and Shia'a opposition groups has so far failed to break the deadlock.[3] In Oman, political changes and promises by Sultan Qaboos following the

2011 protests managed to calm the anger for a while, but without addressing the underlying problems:[4] in 2012, protests erupted again with demands for employment and political reform.[5] In Saudi Arabia, the Saudi government used its official religious establishment to stop mass protests on March 11, 2011. Official religious scholars issued a fatwa denouncing protests. Imams from mosques across the main cities called on people not to destabilize the country.[6] This Saudi strategy has contained the Sunni population, but Saudi Shia citizens continued to protest throughout the following 1 1/2 years.

Saudi Arabia and other GCC states reacted by offering cash handouts and subsidies to their own citizens in order to restrain the transformation of economic malaise into a serious political crisis. King Abdullah of Saudi Arabia cut short his medical rehabilitation stay in Morocco and returned to Riyadh to announce a number of financial packages intended to contain the spread of protests across the country. In February 2011, 19 Royal Orders were announced, including a range of financial support measures such as unemployment benefits, increased wages, a program to build 500,000 housing units, and the writing-off of a series of loans. The total cost of all these social measures over the coming years is estimated to amount to U.S.$130 billion. The unemployment benefit is indicative of the generosity and cost of the measures taken: in an effort to appease the anger of its unemployed youth, the government now provides a year's salary for job-seeking Saudi citizens.[7]

Other GCC states announced similar measures. Bahrain issued a one-off cash transfer of 1000 Bahraini Dinars (approximately U.S.$2,660) per family. Kuwait also gave its own citizens cash handouts of 1000 Kuwaiti Dinars (U.S.$3,500).[8]

Buying legitimacy through public employment, grants, increase of wages, or any other rent distributive tool has proved temporarily effective in some countries, but is unsustainable in the long term, both financially and politically. The rich GCC countries still have a margin of time to keep using the same tactics, because there are abundant financial resources to be mobilized — with budget surpluses accumulated over the last few years, these states still have room for maneuver. But less prosperous Bahrain and Oman cannot continue with this approach at a similar scale to their neighbors. Their populations are aware of this fact, and this is a contributing factor to the continuing protests in these countries, notably absent in the richer states.

But the Story Is Still Unfinished.

The Gulf region has entered a new era. What started as the voicing of socio-economic grievances in GCC states has transformed into a growing political quest for liberties. Local activists are calling for political reforms in almost all countries across the region.

In Saudi Arabia, different political groups (liberals, Islamists, and female groups) are now calling for deep political reforms and liberties. The upheavals across the Arab world have revived calls for a constitutional reform that would transform the Saudi Kingdom into a constitutional monarchy. The constitutional reformists, as they are known, are made up of academics, writers, businessmen, and other professionals of different ideological backgrounds ranging from liberals to pan-Arab nationalists including members of the Islamist Sahwa.[9] Their political reform agenda seeks to curtail the excessive powers held by the King and the royal court. The monarch, according to the Saudi Basic Law, has the power to nominate and dismiss ministers, as well as to dissolve the Consultative Council. He is also the head of the armed forces. Although King Abdullah has set economic and political reforms as priority since his ascent to the throne in 2005, little has changed in political terms. Political reforms were too slow and insubstantial to noticeably change the form of government. In one sense, these were cosmetic reforms, such as a cabinet reshuffle, a change of the head of religious police or the appointment of the first female in the state's history as a deputy minister.[10] The most recent reforms announced by the King, once again intended to undermine any mass build-up of political discontent, are symbolic but once again do not amount to major change: in March 2011, Saudi citizens were granted a right to elect half of the members of municipal councils. Later in the same year, King Abdullah granted women the right to participate in future municipal elections.

There are many conservative forces that oppose meaningful reform in Saudi Arabia, just as they have done successfully in previous decades under the rule of late King Fahd. At the time when King Fahd introduced the first constitution in 1992, several groups voiced opposition for a range of different reasons. The conservative religious establishment saw in the constitution a challenge to the legal order that is based on the Quran. Another opposing group was made up of influential conservative princesses, who did not want to cede any political powers to other institutions. Their main concern was that the adoption of a constitution could set a precedent, and open the door for more substantial political concessions toward a participatory political system.[11] King Fahd was against the organization of free elections in his country, saying that "our people's character and way of life are different from the ways and traditions of the democratic world... free elections are not suitable for our country."[12] These conservative forces are still shaping policy-making in the royal court.

It is not only secular groups that are calling for representative politics; some Islamist groups and activists are now joining the call. The proponents of democracy in Saudi Arabia call for a change from the current political system based on patronage, where princes of the family of Al-Saud dominate key central, regional, and sectoral positions. More significantly, criticism of the current situation and calls for democratic reform are now coming from within the Al-Saud family itself. The old reformist princes are now demanding democratic reforms, and calling on Saudi leaders to initiate reforms to avoid the destiny of deposed leaders elsewhere in the Arab world. For instance, the current King's brother, Prince Talal bin Abdel Aziz, urged the introduction of substantial political reforms to avoid mass uprisings among Saudis.[13] Princess Basma bint Saud bin Abdul Aziz voiced criticism of the entourage of the King for exploiting the authoritarian political system to repress protestors.[14] Turki Al-Hamad, a Saudi author and novelist, eloquently summarized the reform demands in a prologue to a newly published book, titled *The Alternative Saudi: Features of the Fourth State*, written by Ahmad Adnan, a Saudi journalist based in Beirut. He urged the ruling elite to reform in order to avoid being forced to change, adding that calls for reform are not a luxury demand, but rather a necessity.[15]

The current political situation in Bahrain is far more complex. The political tensions between the ruling elite and opposition Shia forces have reached a stale-mate. Shia riots continue at the time of writing. The failure of political dialogue is a consequence of a lack of a united opposition front on the one hand, and of a divided ruling family on the other. A wide gap exists between opposition groups on the scope of ambition for the political reforms wanted for the country.[16] The main opposition group, Alwefaq, is hoping to alter the ruling system by empowering the parliament. On the institutional front, Alwefaq demands a constitutional amendment that gives more powers to parliament to scrutinize all government policies. Some opposition groups have gone further, asking for the removal of the long-serving prime minister, Sheikh Khalifa Al-Khalifa, as a key part of any political settlement. The Sheikh is considered by the Shia population to be a hardliner and an opponent of any political dialogue or concessions.[17] Even more radical groups have called for a total change of the state system, from a monarchy to a republic.

Even in the rich UAE, an opposition Islamist group, the Reform and Social Guidance Association (hereafter Al-Islah), has emerged to call for democratic reforms. In 2011, Al-Islah issued a petition to introduce more pro-democracy reforms. This group has asked for leg-islative powers to be assigned to the Federal National Council, and for voting rights to be given to all citi-zens. Alarmed by this political development, the UAE government reacted firmly and arrested several activ-ists,[18] primarily Islamists. In addition to their calls for the democratization of the system, these Islamists ap-pear to espouse a social project centered on preserving local traditional and conservative culture. A growing number of Emiratis are unsatisfied with the indecent behavior of expatriate residents and tourists in public.

In June 2012, the Federal National Council proposed a dress code law to the cabinet.[19] But the authorities, particularly in Dubai, are concerned about the growth and spread of any moralization discourse within the country, as a trend of this kind would challenge the core of Dubai's business model as a tourist and international business hub. Frequent media statements by Dubai police chief Dahi Khalfan reflects the anxiety among Dubai's leadership about the rise of the Islamic political discourse. Meanwhile, a Dubai-based Emirati academic has noted that while these movements have surprised the leadership, they are unlikely to constitute any threat to the political system.[20] In his view, given the lack of political activism combined with a general satisfaction with the socio-economic conditions among nationals, Al-Islah or any other opposition group will only achieve limited support.[21]

Fear of the Rise of Political Islam.

The political transitions in Egypt and Tunisia have brought in new challenges for the GCC's conservative regimes. They have changed the political landscape in the region by democratically bringing political Islam into power. The victory of the Muslim Brotherhood in Egypt, in particular, was perceived as an unwelcome development. The GCC rulers are alarmed by the potential influence of the Egyptian democratic experience on their own societies. The horrifying scenario for the GCC rulers is if the Egyptian government led by the Muslim Brotherhood decides to spread its influence regionally by empowering other Islamist groups. Abdulakhaleq Abdullah, an Emirati political scientist, notes that the GCC are part and parcel of the Arab world, and they cannot escape the influence of the revolutions and the political transitions that follow them.[22] For instance, the UAE, as with other GCC countries, remain concerned about possible links between their local Islamist groups and other Islamists in power in Tunisia, Morocco and Egypt.

Such fears about a pan-Arab Islamist nexus or influence are not groundless. During a visit by the chairman of Al-Islah, Sultan bin Kaid al-Qassimi, to the Moroccan ruling Islamist Party of Justice and Development, Al-Qassimi stated that the aim of his visit was to learn from Morocco's unique experience of Islamist government in the Arab region.[23]

Sectarian Frictions.

Another internal source of political fragility in several GCC states is the Shia-Sunni split. Shia populations are an integral part of the GCC societies. With the exception of Bahrain, where Shi'ites account for almost 70 percent of the population, in the rest of the GCC states Shia constitutes an important minority. Despite their significant size and centuries of their existence in the region, most of the current Sunni regimes perceive Shi'ism as a threat to their political stability and to social cohesion. This has manifested in systematic discrimination against Shia citizens in most GCC countries by the state apparatuses; Shi'ites are often treated as "second-class" citizens. According to one study on the subject, Shia has not enjoyed proper representation in the civilian or military institutions in the majority of GCC countries. Even in countries that allowed the participation of Shia citizens in managing the state's affairs, they have never breached the ceiling that separates them from the Sunni elite.[24]

There is a wide conviction that the Saudi government has a deliberate policy of discrimination against its Shia subjects. The Saudi authorities deny their Shia subjects the freedom to practice many of their religious ceremonies. Statements by Saudi Sunni clerics that overtly incite discrimination and intolerance against Shia are not prohibited or punished. A 2009 report by Human Rights Watch listed a few examples of institutional discrimination against the Saudi Shia minority, including the dominance of Sunni tribunals over the only three Shia courts and the fact that Saudi schools only teach Sunni Islam to pupils.[25]

The fall of Saddam Hussein's regime in Iraq and the empowerment of Iraqi Shia politicians have brought new dynamics into the region, potentially no less important than the impact of Iran's Islamic revolution in 1979. This change fundamentally altered the geopolitical environment, giving much room to Iranian influence in the Middle East, and the reemergence of Shi'ism across the Gulf and Levant regions. Iranian support of Shia factions in Iraq over recent years has only given weight to the already existing perception that Iran is extending its influence across the region. The concern for the GCC regimes is to once again face outbreaks of Shia revolts, similar to the ones experienced after the Iranian Islamic revolution. A study of political violence related to Shi'ism notes that "since the revolution of 1979, Shia politics and activism in Saudi Arabia has typically been characterized as inspired, influenced and even directed by Iran."[26] This accentuates a common perception among Sunnis in the region that Shia groups of the Gulf are Persians (Aajams) who retain allegiance to Iran. The reality is different; the majority of the GCC's Shia populations are Arabs.

The study cited above suggests that sectarian rivalry will lead to a deteriorating situation:

> In the coming years, Shias and Sunnis will compete over power, first in Iraq but ultimately across the entire region. Beyond Iraq, other countries (even as they embrace reform) have to cope with intensifying rivalries between Shias and Sunnis. The overall Sunni-Shia conflict will play a large role in defining the Middle East as a whole and shaping its relations with the outside world.[27]

It appears that GCC rulers are taking this danger entirely seriously. Saudi Arabia is leading Arab-Sunni governments in a war against a Shia "invasion" of the GCC and the rest of the Middle East. This stance chosen by Saudi Arabia is driven by both geopolitics and ideological factors. On the religious front, the Al-Saud regime is committed to this policy as a result of the great influence of the official religious institutions on policy making. Given the important status of Wahhabism in the Saudi political system, anti-Shi'ism is built into the structure of political and religious authority and has become pervasive in cultural and social institutions. The Saudi education system, for example, has historically preached intolerance for religious views that diverge from core Wahhabi tenets.

The continued alienation of Shia citizens within most GCC societies has structurally damaged the political legitimacy of the rulers and the social cohesion. The magnitude of this sectarian rift has been described eloquently:

> Shia-Sunni conflict . . . has been far more important in shaping the Middle East than many realize or acknowledge. And it has become deeply embedded in

popular prejudice, as stereotypes of the plebeian Shias and their wrongheaded view of Islam have defined how many Sunnis have seen their kinsmen. In Lebanon, popular lore has held that Shias have tails; they reproduce too prolifically, are too loud in expressing their religiosity, and, given Lebanon's debonair self-image, are ridiculed for their low-class, tasteless and vulgar ways. Despite the political popularity of Hezbollah, Shias face discrimination and are dismissed as provincial, uncouth, and unfit for their lofty pretention of representing Lebanon. In Saudi Arabia, it is said that Shia spit in their food — a slander no doubt meant to discourage even socialization over meals between Sunnis and Shias — and that shaking hands with a Shia is polluting, necessitating ablutions.[28]

The Sunni-Shia rifts are most acute now in Bahrain and Saudi Arabia. This has been the case for both countries for decades; both have seen several bouts of religious upheaval since the Islamic revolution in Iran in 1979. The religious divide has become even more pronounced in the two countries over the last 1 1/2 years, and the local authorities appear to be struggling to address it. By contrast, other GCC countries have adopted a conciliatory approach toward Shia groups.

Succession Issues.

Another threat to internal stability lies in the infighting within the ruling families for positions of influence in most GCC countries. Such confrontations are exacerbated by a lack of clear rules for successions, and the complete absence of strong democratic institutions. The succession in Saudi Arabia, for instance, remains uncertain, and this is perceived as a potential source of political instability by many observers. Recently, the death of two crown princes, Sultan and

Nayef, in less than a year brought to the fore questions over the regime's stability in the mid and long term.[29] The vagueness of the succession system introduced by King Abdullah in 2006 leaves the matter unresolved once the aging and unwell sons of King Abdul Aziz die. There are dozens of contenders among the grandsons for the throne, with the strong possibility of factional disputes.[30]

Even in other GCC countries that have clearer stipulations for selecting successors, political systems characterized by family rule precipitate political uncertainty. The competition for senior positions is fierce. A recent example to illustrate how confusing and risky the situation could be is the succession dispute in the Ras Al-Khaima Emirate of the UAE. When the late Sheikh Saqr Al-Qassimi died in October 2010, two of his sons, Khalid and Saud, contended for the throne with their competition causing a political crisis in the UAE as a whole.[31]

EXTERNAL THREATS TO GCC STABILITY

A Dangerous Neighbor: Mounting Tensions with Iran.

Arab Gulf countries have several concerns about Iran. First, they suspect that Iran is directly supporting Shia minorities, which is considered as direct interference in their domestic affairs. Second, Iran has continually criticized the strong ties between some Arab governments and the United States. Iran is anxious about the U.S. presence in the region,[32] and the presence of foreign forces in the Gulf region has consequently increased other states' fears of Iran.[33] Third, there are territorial disputes with several GCC members, and Gulf rulers remain concerned about expansionist intentions of the Iranian regime.

There is also a deeper and broader underlying source of animosity. Iran's desire to become a regional power constitutes a source of fear to its immediate Arab neighbors and other world powers. According to a 2011 study:

> Iran believes that it ought to play a major role in world affairs and that, as the defender of the interests of all Muslims and the guardian of Iran's national interests, it should be treated as a beacon for revolutionary Islam throughout the world. Finally . . . its leadership's belief [is] that Iran is geographically optimally situated to become the dominant power in the Persian Gulf.[34]

The mistrust of Iran by GCC countries has deepened over the last decade. The U.S.-led war on Iraq in 2003 profoundly changed the regional balance of power: Iran emerged as the dominant force in the region following the collapse of Saddam Hussein's regime. Since then, as mentioned earlier, the GCC countries have been alarmed over pro-Iran Shi'ites gaining power in post-war Iraq and threatening to extend Shia influence across the region. In fact, the rise of Shia in Iraq has encouraged other Shia minorities in the region to aspire to greater prominence in their respective countries. But it is important to note that the underlying enmity stretches back decades. The tensions between Iran and most GCC countries have historical, ideological, and geostrategic roots, which make their animosity a structural feature rather than a cyclical one that depends on the ascendancy of hardline political factions in the Iranian politics or the accession to power of a new Arab monarch.

The full complexities of the relationships between Iran and its Arab Gulf neighbors cannot be covered exhaustively in a monograph of this size, but a brief review can be given of some specific issues and how they are linked to the ongoing tensions in the region.[35] Arab Gulf countries have perceived Iran as a threat since before their independence. The enshrined sense of superiority among Iranian nationalists since the time of the Shahs stokes this animosity. This sense of superiority, which contrasts with the relative modesty of Arab neighbors, is based on Persian glorification of their pre-Islamic era.[36] The overthrow of Shah Reza Pahlavi in 1979 fundamentally altered the region's geopolitical landscape for the Arab countries and other external Western powers. For the Arab countries, the change of regime brought a clerical system that was hostile to the Sunni regimes and monarchies of the Gulf region. For the United States, the Islamic revolution removed a key ally in the region.

Iran's territorial disputes with its Arab neighbors in the Gulf also go back to before the Islamic revolution. Iranian claims on Bahrain in particular date back to the British announcement of withdrawal from the Gulf region in 1968.[37] Calls from leading Iranian political figures and public opinion formers, but not the government, to annex Bahrain have intensified over recent years. Iran's opposition to any deep integration among Arab Gulf countries only reinforces these fears. In July 2007, Hossein Shariatmadari, the editor of *Kayhan*, a daily newspaper that is known to be close to conservative political circles, revived Iran's claim to Bahrain. His comments sparked a diplomatic crisis in Bahrain.[38] Again in 2009, Ali Akbar Nateq Nouri, a prominent politician and a member of Iran's Expediency Council, alluded to such claims.[39] The Iranian government has always distanced itself from such provocative statements and claims. In May 2012, Iran was alarmed by Riyadh-Manama talks over the potential establishment of a political union, and saw in this initiative a potential game-changer that could challenge its influence and leadership ambitions in the region. The Saudi announcement intensified a war of words between Iranian and GCC institutions. The Iranian parliament voiced its disapproval of the proposed closer political relationship, and the suggestion by Ali Larijani, speaker of the Iranian parliament, that if Bahrain should have any merger at all it should be with Iran provoked a strong Bahraini official reaction.[40] Bahrain's foreign ministry summoned the Iranian Chargé d'Affaires to complain against what they described as Iranian interference in Bahrain's internal affairs. This is not the first time that Iranian claims on Bahrain have collided with a desire for political integration: Iran opposed Bahrain's attempts to join the Trucial States Federation in the early 1970s, and then successfully opposed Bahrain's accession to the UAE federation — in both cases because of the view that Bahrain is properly Iranian territory.[41]

The UAE have not relinquished their claims on three islands(Abu Musa and the Tunbs) that were annexed by Iran in 1971, following the British departure, and have continued to reassert their claim to them at United Nations (UN) meetings ever since. The Iranian argument is that these islands had belonged to Iran before falling into the hands of the Arab Sheikhs of Ras Al-Khaima and Sharjah with the help of Britain.[42] The UAE government stance has not changed, maintaining a call on the Iranian authorities to either negotiate bilaterally or refer their dispute to the International Court of Justice. Iran is disinclined to negotiate over the sovereignty of the three islands.

Maritime delimitation between Kuwait and Saudi Arabia also remains a pending issue. The disputed maritime territory is rich in hydrocarbon resources, which increases its geopolitical importance. The Arash, also known as al-Dorra, an offshore gas field shared between Kuwait, Saudi Arabia, and Iran, is believed to possess substantial reserves estimated at 200 billion cubic meters. In addition to the potential natural resources, extending the territorial water of Iran means maximizing its powers as a coastal state in a vital sea passage, as vessels departing the region would have to report to the Iranian authorities. Iran would acquire more powers to apply its environmental laws and restrict the movement of external military forces. In recent months, the dispute over maritime space and the joint field resurfaced when Iran announced in January 2012 its intentions to unilaterally develop the al-Dorra field. Given the need to increase gas production, all three countries are keen to develop the joint-field as soon as possible. But the possibility of joint exploration and development depends first upon the demarcation of maritime borders and furthermore on the regional political situation.

For all these factors listed above, Arab Gulf-Iranian relations have experienced many instances of tensions and hostilities over at least the last 5 decades. Not surprisingly, these tensions may intensify in the immediate future.

The Iranian Threat—Nuclear Issues and Blockade.

Iran's aspiration to develop a nuclear capability is an additional specific issue that adds to tensions in the region. Concerns about real Iranian nuclear plans have alarmed the GCC states and Western powers.

Despite Iran's continuous assertion that its aim is to develop civilian nuclear capability, GCC governments remain skeptical about its genuine goal. Iran's obscure attitude on the nuclear issue only reinforces anxiety among the Arab countries and across the world. Official statements suggest that the GCC leaders have opted for a conciliatory approach on Iran's nuclear issue. In December 2011, Dubai's ruler and the UAE Prime Minister Sheikh Mohammed Bin Rashid Al-Maktoum, in an interview with CNN, played down fears over Iran's plans to develop nuclear weapons. He said that Iran is a Muslim country, and "[W]e have lived next to each other for thousands and thousands of years. I don't believe that Iran will develop a nuclear weapon." Public opinion on the issue among GCC leaders is almost unanimous. Their core message is a desire to curtail Iran's nuclear program in a peaceful way. They call on the international community to use dialogue and diplomacy, not military strikes, to handle the issue. Their views are well-presented in a GCC Secretariat General statement that followed the GCC Supreme Council meeting in 2009. The statement reiterates the aim of the GCC leaders to have a nuclear-free region, and further reads that:

> The Supreme Council hailed international efforts aimed at solving the Iranian nuclear crisis through diplomatic means, and expressed hope that all concerned sides would reach a political settlement that would eliminate the fears and doubts on the nature of this dossier, [and] bring about peace and stability in the region.[43]

However, although GCC officials are overtly less confrontational on the Iranian nuclear program compared to Israel and Western powers, they remain concerned about the repercussions of a nuclear Iran. The statements of semi-officials may be an indication of GCC countries' private views on the issue. The Saudi Prince Turki Al-Faisal, who leads the King Faisal Centre for Research and Islamic Studies, has frequently commented on the issue since he left his post as Ambassador to Washington. In January 2012, Turki Al-Faisal warned the world that any failure to stop Iran from developing nuclear weapons could lead to a nuclear arms race in the Middle East, which would make a volatile region even worse. Given a nuclear Iran, countries like Saudi Arabia, Egypt, Iraq, and Algeria among others would prefer to possess their own nuclear capabilities as a deterrent against their neighbor.[44] In 2008, Sami Al-Faraj, director of the Kuwait Centre for Strategy Studies and a former government advisor, expressed support for an Israeli attack on Iran's nuclear facilities.[45] A nuclear-armed Iran would have enduring ramifications for the stability of the GCC political regimes and balance of power in the entire Middle East. But support for the use of force against Iran by Western or Israeli forces on the part of actual GCC leaders is likely to be tempered by the likelihood of Iranian reprisals against U.S. military and other facilities in their own countries, with the strong likelihood of collateral damage.

Another example that encapsulates the diplomatic dissimulation practiced by some GCC regimes toward Iran is a public statement by a senior UAE diplomat in 2010 that provoked a row between Iran and the UAE. Youssed Al-Otaiba, the UAE Ambassador in Washington, was quoted in a conference suggesting that a preemptive military strike on Iran's nuclear facilities would be cheaper than living with a nuclear Iran in the future. The UAE Foreign Ministry reacted immediately asserting that the UAE government's stance remains unchanged, supporting a peaceful solution to the Iran nuclear issue.[46] With the nuclear question not featuring in talks between GCC countries and Iran, it would appear that the GCC leaders have left the issue to other members of the international community to deal with.

Iran's secrecy and lack of constructive engagement with the international community have failed to foster confidence over its intentions. A report by the International Atomic Energy Agency (IAEA) in 2011 raised concerns that undisclosed Iranian nuclear activities suggest that Iran is developing the technologies to acquire nuclear weapons.[47] The report supported the widely-held view that Iran is deceiving the international community about its nuclear plans.

Less dramatically, but potentially of equal significance, Iranian threats to disrupt free passage through the Strait of Hormuz have intensified over the last few years. With most of the region's oil and liquified natural gas (LNG) exports passing through the Strait, the threats aim to pressure both the Arab Gulf countries, and the major economies that import their energy from the region. In fact, over one-third of all petroleum traded by sea globally passes through the Strait.[48] Any blockade of the Strait of Hormuz would constitute a serious threat to the GCC economy and stability, not only because of oil exports, but because the region also depends on imports of food, and any obstruction of shipments could rapidly lead to severe food shortages and internal instability.

Iran—GCC Policy.

The GCC countries have no unified foreign policy toward Iran, despite their common anxiety about the Iranian aspirations for regional hegemony. There are different foreign policy stances. Saudi Arabia has followed a confrontational policy toward Iran, at least since the 1979 Islamic revolutions, when the late Ayatollah Khomeini had been hostile toward the Saudi ruling family, publicly inciting Saudis to overthrow the Al-Saudi family. The hegemonic competition over influence in the Arab world is another explanation for Saudi Arabia's confrontational stance; both countries have been engaged in proxy conflicts in Lebanon, Iraq, and currently Syria. Bahrain's relationship with Iran suffers from enduring tensions as a result of the Iranian sovereignty claims on Bahrain. Relations were also further damaged by Iran's continuing commentary on Bahrain's Shia situation, which is perceived by the Bahraini regime as interference in its internal affairs. Other GCC small countries have opted for a pragmatic approach in their relations with Iran, with foreign policies driven by national interests rather than by any ideology or hegemonic ambitions. Unresolved territorial disputes have not stopped UAE and Qatar from maintaining good economic relations with Iran.

Oman in particular follows a different approach in its relations with Iran, attaching great importance to stabilizing and strengthening ties. Positive relations between the two countries pre-date Iran's 1979 revolution, with Sultan Qaboos expressing gratitude for the military support of Iran (along with Britain) during the Dhofar war in the mid-1970s.[49] Oman's foreign policy vis-à-vis Iran is driven by its national interests and by no means follows the stance of Saudi Arabia or any other powers. The fundamental assumptions driving this stance are that first, Oman does not share the hegemonic ambitions of Saudi Arabia, and second, Oman sees Iran as a natural security and economic partner because of its geographic proximity and economic size. The fact that both states are littoral countries to the Strait of Hormuz naturally gives rise to common interests in regional security cooperation.

Over the years, both countries have invested in developing their relations in all sectors, and during a visit to Tehran in 2009, Sultan Qaboos signed a number of economic and security agreements. Iran is an important trade partner for Oman[50] — in 2011, Iran was the third largest importer of Omani exports.[51] Bilateral relations extend into strategically significant spheres. Under an agreement signed in August 2012, Oman plans to import natural gas from Iran to meet its growing demand. The two countries hold regular military meetings and exercises, and Oman has committed to refuse to engage in military alliances against Iran. In February 2012, the Omani-Iranian Military Committee convened its tenth meeting to discuss regional security and cooperation.[52] Another example of the healthy state of relations is the Oman Foreign Ministry handling consular issues for the closed Iranian embassy in London.[53]

It is important to note that these differences in foreign policy across the GCC toward Iran show a balance between tactical priorities and a desire to protect the region's territorial integrity and long-term interests. A failure to back the Saudi approach in dealing with Iran may not be well received in Riyadh, but has not been a cause of any public rift, so far, among officials.

GCC Stability: Implications for the United States.

The GCC's geographic location, hydrocarbon, and financial wealth are and will remain of great strategic importance to U.S. interests and security. The GCC countries have abundant oil and natural gas reserves that are of great importance to U.S. economic prosperity and security. Continuing high oil prices for almost a decade now have allowed GCC states to accumulate in aggregate almost U.S.$1 trillion in foreign currency reserves.

The United States has been the main guarantor of stability and security in the Gulf region since the early 1970s, following the withdrawal of the British from east of Suez. During this period, a number of GCC countries have established security cooperation agreements with the United States, leading to basing rights for Army and other U.S. military units. In addition to basing and transit, U.S. forces regularly carry out joint exercises with and offer training to GCC military forces. To counter the increasing challenges posed by Iran in the region, the U.S. Army is planning to strengthen its presence in Kuwait and deploy more ground forces there and potentially to other GCC member countries.[54] These bilateral security ties between the region and the United States are to be the subject of a further monograph to be published by the Strategic Studies Institute in 2013.

Undoubtedly, potential Iranian dominance in the region is a threat to U.S. national interests in the GCC area and the remainder of the Middle East. The current Iranian regime aspires to extend its influence both within the region and beyond. Iran's threats emanate from its ideological beliefs, which not only contradict but also aim to undermine U.S. values and interests in the region and beyond. Iranian revolutionary clerics have openly asserted their objective of extending the Islamic revolution throughout the Middle East and North African region as well as to counter perceived American imperialism around the world.

U.S. interests are best preserved by a balance between different power centers amongst GCC states and in the wider Middle East. A monopoly of excessive power by any one country would not be a desirable outcome. The rise of a sole regional power could risk the region's stability and consequently U.S. national interests. The United States and Western allies should aim to prevent the fall of the region's oil and gas reserves under the influence of any single hegemonic power.

The two key benefits for the United States for peace and stability in the region are the security of energy supply and freedom of movement for the U.S. military. From an oil market perspective, the spare capacity of GCC major oil producers, Saudi Arabia, Kuwait, and Abu Dhabi, is critical for world oil supplies and prices. During the Libyan civil war in 2011, it was the increased output of three GCC countries that compensated for Libya's disrupted production. The Strait of Hormuz is vital both for the GCC and for the world economy, with 90 percent of Middle Eastern oil and LNG exports passing through the Straits. Freedom of movement and an unchallenged presence in the region are key for a range of ongoing tasks for the U.S. Army and other services. Sudden regime change could occur in any GCC state due to internal political turmoil, and this could replace current regimes supportive of U.S. presence with a far less well-disposed environment. An unexpected shift in support from the GCC states could increase the cost of presence and potentially limit options for supply and transport in and out of the U.S. military's theater of operations as logistical plans are forming for post-2014 withdrawal of U.S. combat troops from Afghanistan. In a worst case scenario, political instability leading to sudden regime change to an unfriendly or even hostile regime could cause severe disruption in U.S. plans for wide scale drawdown of U.S. troops and equipment, or even potentially pose a new and direct challenge to the U.S. military in the Gulf.

U.S. policymakers should therefore consider the implications and options listed below for fostering continued stability in the region and preempting internal and international developments that could threaten the current balance of power.

POLICY IMPLICATIONS AND RECOMMENDATIONS

There are several policy implications and recommendations that proceed from this analysis.

- The Arab Spring has brought fundamental changes to the GCC geostrategic landscape. The transformation is still unfolding, and the strategic consequences for GCC societies and regimes could be far reaching. This in turn has important implications for regional stability and hence for key U.S. interests in GCC states.
- Political volatility, including that caused by the Sunni-Shia divide, affects support for U.S. interests and presence in the region.
- The U.S. Army requires freedom of movement in the Gulf for a range of purposes, including logistical support to deployed forces, as a primary training and forward deployment

hub, and to support withdrawal from Iraq and Afghanistan.

- The option of use of the GCC region for reverse transit from Afghanistan both before and after 2014 is especially important for reducing reliance on the Northern Distribution Network (NDN), including for the withdrawal of sensitive cargoes, which it would be inappropriate to ship by ground transport through Central Asia and Russia. Loss of freedom of movement in the GCC area would render the withdrawal process hostage to political goodwill in NDN transit countries.
- In light of increased tensions and threats to the stability of the region, the U.S. Army should increase its training programs to strengthen and modernize the kinetic capabilities of the GCC militaries. These training undertakings are not one-sided; frequent contacts with GCC officers strengthen communication between U.S. and local Army forces. The U.S. Army could also share essential nonkinetic skills with their counterparts in the GCC countries, in particular to strengthen their capabilities in dealing with chemical, biological, and nuclear containments.
- Political change toward more participatory democracy and accountability in the region is an irreversible process. The GCC regimes should be encouraged to adopt substantial changes to their political systems as a whole, rather than limit themselves to topical or cosmetic changes for populist effect, in order to avoid the danger of mass upheavals and an uncontrolled transition of power that risks the arrival of an unpredictable successor regime unfriendly to U.S. interests and presence.

- Maintaining U.S. presence across the region is crucial not only to U.S. interests there, but also for the GCC states themselves. U.S. presence not only guarantees the security of GCC states against external threats such as Iran or other global emerging powers, but also provides each small GCC state with protection against Saudi hegemonic ambitions in the region. Shared U.S. and GCC interests in an enduring U.S. presence provides the United States not only with a range of strategic options for assuring U.S. interests in the region, but also with the additional benefit of flexibility and leverage in relations with individual GCC states in the interests of maintaining strategic balance and good relations.

CONCLUSION

As time passes, calls for participatory governance and greater transparency will increase and spread among broad segments of the GCC societies, including the small prosperous Gulf monarchies. There are a number of intertwined factors that serve as signposts toward this socio-political development. First, increased education and political awareness among the population—particularly the youth, the growing numbers of whom have attended Western universities, mainly in Anglo-Saxon societies, and thus have been exposed to the democratic values and institutions of Western societies. Although this does not mean that they will become militant for political change in their own societies immediately, this is knowledge and experience that will shape their thinking and political aspirations. Second, the wave of political transformation that is sweeping across the region has been far from unnoticed in the GCC societies. Once the political transitions in Tunisia, Egypt, and Libya have crystallized into defined, institutionalized, and functioning models, the way will be shown for GCC states and societies to follow suit.

ENDNOTES

1. Formally the Cooperation Council for the Arab States of the Gulf (CCASG), comprised of Bahrain, Kuwait, Oman, Qatar, Saudi Arabia, and the UAE. Jordan and Morocco are under consideration as potential members.

2. ASDA'A Burson-Marsteller, "Third Annual ASDA'A Burson-Marsteller Arab Youth Survey," March 15, 2011, available from *www.arabyouthsurvey.com/2010/files/AYS2010_Top_10_Findings_Top_5_Findings_2011.pdf*.

3. Jane Kinninmont, "Bahrain: Beyond the Impasse," *Chatham house*, June 2012, available from *www.chathamhouse.org/sites/default/files/public/Research/Middle%20East/pr0612kinninmont.pdf*.

4. "Omanis Protest in Sign of Renewed Discontent," *Gulf News*, July 2, 2012, available from *gulfnews.com/news/gulf/oman/omanis-protest-in-sign-of-renewed-discontent-1.1043396*.

5. "Oman: Waking up Too," *The Economist*, June 23, 2012, available from *www.economist.com/node/21557354*.

6. Madawi Al-Rasheed, "No Saudi Spring: Anatomy of a Failed Revolution," *Boston Review*, March/April 2012, available from *www.bostonreview.net/BR37.2/madawi_al-rasheed_arab_spring_saudi_arabia.php*.

7. Ulrike Freitag, "Saudi Arabia: Buying Stability?" Muriel Asseburg, ed., *Protest, Revolt, and Regime Change in the Arab World: Actors, Challenges, Implications, and Policy Options, SWP Research Paper*, Berlin, Germany: German Institute of International and Security Affairs, February 2012, available from *www.swp-berlin.org/fileadmin/contents/products/research_papers/2012_RP06_ass.pdf*.

8. James Calderwood, "Kuwait Gives each Citizen DH 13,000 and Free Food," *The National*, January 18, 2011, available from *www.thenational.ae/news/world/middle-east/kuwait-gives-each-citizen-dh13-000-and-free-food*.

9. Madawi Al-Rasheed, "Mashru'a Thadith al-hukm al-sa'audi" ("Project of Reforming the Saudi Government"), *Al-Mustakbal Al-Arabi Magazine*, No. 368, October 2009, pp. 102-133.

10. Ana Echague, "Saudi Arabia: Supply-Side Reform?" *FRIDE*, Policy Brief No. 15, July 2009.

11. Rashed Aba-Namay, "The Recent Constitutional Reforms in Saudi Arabia," *The International and Comparative Law Quarterly*, Vol. 42, No. 2, April 1993, pp. 295-331.

12. Rashed Aba-Namay, "The New Saudi Representative Assembly," *Islamic Law and Society*, Vol. 5, Issue 2, 1998, pp. 235-265.

13. Mourad Haroutunian, "Saudi Prince Says Protests May Move to the Kingdom, BBC Arabic Says," *Bloomberg*, February 18, 2011, available from *www.bloomberg.com/news/2011-02-18/saudi-prince-says-protests-may-move-to-kingdom-bbc-arabic-says.html*.

14. Cahal Milmo, "The Acton Princess Calling for Reform in Saudi Arabia," *The Independent*, January 30, 2012, available from *www.independent.co.uk/news/people/news/the-acton-princess-calling-for-reform-in-saudi-arabia-6284225.html*.

15. Ahmad Adnan, "Adawla Al-sa'udiya: malamih al-dawla al-rabia'a" ("The Saudi State: Features of the Fourth State"), Beirut, Lebanon: Altanweer Press, 2012, pp. 10-16.

16. Reza H. Akbari, "Bahrain's Triangle of Conflict," *Foreign Policy*, May 17, 2012, available from *mideast.foreignpolicy.com/posts/2012/05/17/bahrains_triangle_of_conflict*.

17. Roula Khalaf, "West Urged to Back Change in Bahrain," *The Financial Times*, December 13, 2011, available from *www.ft.com/cms/s/0/45bef9d2-2595-11e1-9c76-00144feabdc0.html#axzz1kH189PLn*.

18. Angela Shah, "Emirates Step-up Efforts to Counter Dissent," *The New York Times*, May 30, 2012, available from *www.nytimes.com/2012/05/31/world/middleeast/united-arab-emirates-step-up-efforts-to-counter-dissent.html*.

19. Jay B. Hilotin, "FNC Members Seek Penalties for Flouting Dress Code," *Gulf News*, June 14, 2012, available from *gulfnews.com/news/gulf/uae/fnc-member-seeks-penalties-for-flouting-dress-code-1.1035715*.

20. An interview conducted by the author in London, UK, on July 10, 2012.

21. Mohammed Aaz Al-Aarab, "Intikhabat al-majlis al-wataniwa al-Islah al-siyasi fi al-imarat" ("Election in the National Council and Political Reform in the Emirates"), *Al-Ahram Digital*, November 2011, available from *digital.ahram.org.eg/articles.aspx?Serial=858878&eid=7887*.

22. Abdulkhaleq Abdullah, "Repercussions of the Arab Spring on GCC States," Research Paper, Arab Centre for Research and Policy Studies, May 2012.

23. Mohamed Laghrous, "Hiwarma'a Shaykh sultan al-kassimi, ra'isjam'iyat al-islahwa al-tawjih al-ijtima'I" ("Interview with Sheikh Sultan Al-Qassimi, Chairman of Reform and Social Guidance"), *Attawhidwal-Islah Movement*, available from *alislah.ma/2009-10-07-11-53-04/item/21727.html*.

24.Vali Nasr, *The Shia Revival: How Conflicts within Islam Will Shape the Future*, London, UK: W. W. Norton & Company, 2007, pp. 92-93.

25. Human Rights Watch, "Denied Dignity: Systematic Discrimination and Hostility toward Saudi Shia Citizens," September 2009, pp. 10-12.

26. Toby Jones, "Saudi Arabia" Assaf Moghadam, ed., *Political Violence: Militancy and Political Violence in Shiism: Trends and Patterns*, Florence, KY: Routledge, 2011, p. 136.

27. Nasr, p. 24.

28. *Ibid.*, pp. 22-23.

29. Abeer Allam, "Death Highlights Saudi Succession Problem," *The Financial Times*, June 17, 2012, available from *www.ft.com/intl/cms/s/0/c6dba82e-b86d-11e1-a2d6-00144feabdc0. html#axzz25LNBb8ua.*

30. "The Saudi Succession: When Kings and Princes Grow Old," *The Economist*, July 15, 2010, available from *www.economist. com/node/16588422.*

31. Simeon Kerr, "Rival in Ras al-Khaimah Throne Leaves Emirate," *The Financial Times*, October 28, 2010, available from *www.ft.com/intl/cms/s/0/52ca6982-e2c4-11df-8a58-00144feabdc0. html#axzz25LNBb8ua.*

32. Mahjoob Zweiri, "Arab-Iranian Relations: New Realities?" Anoushiravan Ehteshami and Mahjoob Zweiri, eds., *Iran's Foreign policy: From Khatami to Ahmadinejad*, Reading, UK: Ithaca Press, 2008, pp. 116-117.

33. Mahboubeh Sadeghini, *Security Arrangements in the Persian Gulf: With Special Reference to Iran's Foreign Policy*, Reading, UK: Ithaca Press, 2011, pp. 200-201.

34. Sadeghini, p. 203.

35. Al-Saud, Faisal bin Salman, *Iran, Saudi Arabia and the Gulf: Power Politics in Transition*, London, UK: I. B. Tauris, 2004.

36. Arshin Adib-Moghaddam, *International Politics of the Persian Gulf: a Cultural Genealogy*, Florence, KY: Routledge, 2006, pp. 16-17.

37. Faisal Bin Slaman al-Saud, *Iran, Saudi Arabia, and the Gulf: Power Politics in Transition*, London, UK: I. B. Tauris, 2004, pp. 32-33.

38. Joseph A. Kechichian, "Iran has no Claim to Bahrain," *Gulf News*, July 25, 2007, available from *gulfnews.com/opinions/ columnists/iran-has-no-claim-to-bahrain-1.191112.*

39. Sherine Bahaa, "Is Bahrain Another Kuwait?" *Al-Ahram Weekly*, Issue No. 936, March 4, 2009, available from *weekly.ahram.org.eg/2009/936/re62.htm*.

40. Habib Toumi, "Bahrain Condemns Iran's Interference in its Domestic Affairs," *Gulf News*, May 16, 2012, available from *gulfnews.com/news/gulf/bahrain/bahrain-condemns-iran-s-inter-ference-in-its-domestic-affairs-1.1023774*.

41. Miriam Joyce, *Ruling Shaikhs and Her Majesty's Government, 1960-1969: Britain's Last Decade in the Gulf, the 1960s*, London, UK: Frank Cass Publishers, 2003, pp. 117-119.

42. Ahmad Jalinusi and Vahid Barari Arayee, "The Three Islands: (Abu Musa, The Greater & Lesser Tunb Islands) Integral Parts of Iran," *The Iranian Journal of International Affairs*, Vol. XIX, No. 4, Fall 2007, pp. 1-23.

43. Gulf Cooperation Council Secretariat General, "The Final Communique of the 30th Session," December 14-15, 2009, available from *www.gcc-sg.org/eng/indexce7c.html?action=Sec-Show&ID=303*.

44. Claire Ferris-Lay, "Saudi Prince Warns of Middle East Nuclear Arms Race," *Arabian Business*, January 26, 2012, available from *www.arabianbusiness.com/saudi-prince-warns-of-middle-east-nuclear-arms-race-442448.html*.

45. Associated Press, "Kuwait Analyst for Destruction of Iran N-Plant," *Saudi Gazette*, March 10, 2008, available from *www.saudigazette.com.sa/index.cfm?method=home.regcon&contentid=20080310295*.

46. Ian Black, "UAE Ambassador Backs Strikes on Iran's Nuclear Sites," *The Guardian*, July 7, 2010, available from *www.guardian.co.uk/world/2010/jul/07/uae-envoy-iran-nuclear-sites*.

47. Anthony H. Cordesman, "The New IAEA Report and Iran's Evolving Nuclear and Missile Forces," Washington, DC: Center for Strategic and International Studies, November 8, 2011, available from *csis.org/files/publication/111108_irans_evolving_nuclear_forces.pdf*.

48. "Strait of Hormuz" World Oil Transit Chokepoints, U.S. Energy Information Administration. December 30, 2011, available from *www.eia.gov/countries/regions-topics.cfm?fips=WOTC#hormuz.*

49. Al-Qabas, "Limadatanfaridu Oman bita'amulmaa Iran biKhilafi Shakikatiha?" ("Why Oman's unique dealing with Iran is different from its Sisters?"), October 26, 2010, available from *www.gulfsecurity.org/?p=4495.* See also MERIP, "New Iranian Offensive in Oman," *MERIP Reports,* No. 43, 1975, p. 23.

50. Mohamed Abdulla Mohamed, "Umanwa Iran Ba'ad Ziyarat Jalalat al-sultan" ("Oman and Iran After the Visit of His Majesty the Sultan"), *Alwasat,* No. 2530, August 10, 2009, available from *www.alwasatnews.com/2530/news/read/208068/1.html.*

51. Central Bank of Oman, "Annual Report 2011," June 2011, p. 98, available from *www.cbo-oman.org/.*

52. "Iran-Oman Military Committee Meeting Wraps up: Joint Drills in the Winter.," *Iran Daily,* May 16, 2012, available from *www.iran-daily.com/1391/2/27/MainPaper/4234/Page/2/Main Paper_4234_2.pdf.*

53. Nasser Krimi, "Iran: Tehran and London Agree to Repre-sentation," *Bloomberg Businessweek,* June 28, 2012, available from *www.businessweek.com/ap/2012-06-28/iran-tehran-and-london-for-malize-embassy-closures.*

54. Donna Cassata, "U.S. Plans Significant Military Presence in Kuwait," *The Washington Post,* June 19, 2012, available from *www.washingtontimes.com/news/2012/jun/19/us-plans-significant-military-presence-kuwait/.*

www.ingramcontent.com/pod-product-compliance
Lightning Source LLC
Chambersburg PA
CBHW071327310526
45789CB00016B/1688